Central Otago

NEW ZEALAND

GILBERT VAN REENEN

Published and distributed by
Clean Green Press
a division of
Clean Green Images Ltd,
641 Ballantyne Road,
RD 2, Wanaka 9382,
New Zealand

www.cleangreen.co.nz

© 2004 Gilbert van Reenen

© 2004 Neville Peat

The moral rights of both authors have been asserted.

First edition published 2004
Reprinted 2005
Reprinted 2007
Reprinted 2011

Photographs: Gilbert van Reenen
Introductory text: Neville Peat
Printing: Midas International

ISBN 0 476 00911 1

Also by this author
New Zealand South
The Nature of Wanaka

Next page: Hawkdun Range from above the Lindis Pass

clean green press

Central Otago

NEW ZEALAND

GILBERT VAN REENEN

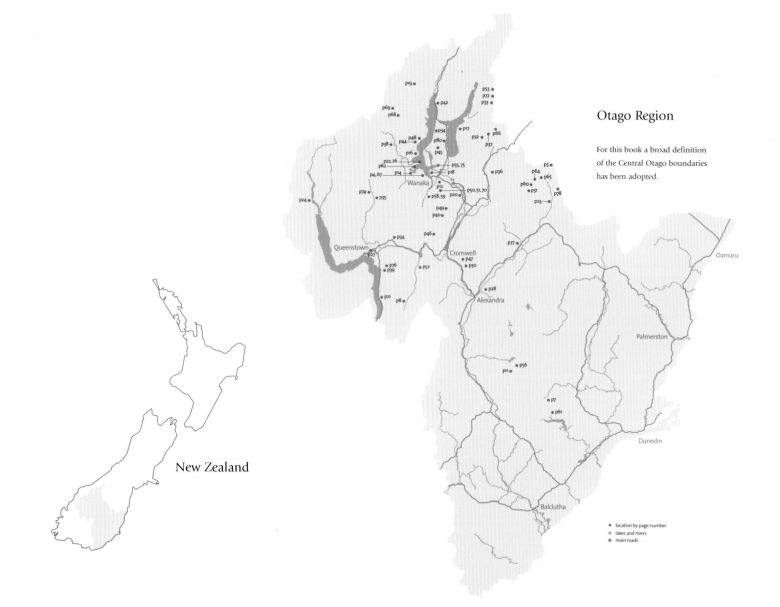

New Zealand

Otago Region

For this book a broad definition of the Central Otago boundaries has been adopted.

p19
p53
p72
p33
p69
p42
p68
p34 p17
p48 p66
p38 p44 p80 p32
p16 p45 p37
p22, 26 p3
p62 p55, 75 p64
p4, 67 p14 p18 p36 p65
Wanaka p60
p12 p31 p78
p74 p50, 51, 70 p23
p35 p58, 59 p20
p24 p49
p40
p54 p46
Queenstown p77
p27 Cromwell
p76 p47
p39 p52 p30
p21 p8
p28
Alexandra
Oamaru

Palmerston

p11 p56

p7
p61

Dunedin

Balclutha

● location by page number
▦ lakes and rivers
■ main roads

East from Lammerlaw Top Te Papanui Conservation Park

Sensual to the point of surreal, Central Otago is an achingly lonely summit crest, a glacial lake gouged to below sea level, muscular mountainsides shimmering with snow tussock in a fohn wind, towering billow clouds, hoar frost filigree, and a rage of autumn colours. Central Otago is a poem, a song, a cry for something lost in time. The landscape, once a paradise for birds, remembers moa of just about every kind, eagles almost too big to fly, imposing adzebills, browsing takahe and mouse-sized bats that crawled about the forest floor at dusk. Flightlessness was the fashion in a land without predatory mammals. Forest and shrubland covered large tracts of this basin-and-range hinterland, which is today swathed in the golden brown of tussock grasses, tall and short, and the gaudy green of irrigated lower country.

Sensual Central

Neville Peat

Gold miners' cottages, Pacteolus claim, Nevis Valley

Central Otago in outline

Among the human symbols here are the mullock heaps and stone cottages of 19th century gold-rushes, and the merinos and fence posts crafted from slabs of schist or ancient totara and kowhai logs that are the mementoes of a pastoral frontier.

There is no place like Central. No New Zealand region has landscape character like this. It is the kind of place that can become deeply etched in a traveller's mind – and a resident's soul.

After eons of a sculpting by freeze-thaw and wind-whip, schist tors ride the rangelands in distinctive style – an obelisk here, a balancing act there, a face, an animal, a test of the imagination. The mountains are built of splintery schist. This rock type started out as sediments laid down under an unrecognisable ocean off embryonic Australia two hundred million years or more ago. Subsequently it was transformed by stupendous squeezing and heating into the metamorphic schist of today. In New Zealand, Central Otago bears a mother-lode of this rock.

A byproduct of its formation is gold – hence the region's history of sluicing, mining and dredging. Sluicing pursued the fragments of gold released into water courses by natural erosion; the early miners dug adits and shafts to access gold-bearing quartz reefs; and huge floating dredges churned through river beds and adjacent terraces chasing the gold remnants. The Otago gold rushes, which followed those of California and Victoria in Australia were of world significance, and many nationalities arrived to try their luck.

The pattern of settlement today, including the arterial roading, was largely determined by gold, with towns like Queenstown, Arrowtown, Alexandra and Cromwell, and villages like St Bathans, Ophir, and Naseby all built on backs of the gold diggers.

In the 1860s and 1870s, Otago took in Southland, Fiordland and Stewart Island. These days it is smaller but a large region nonetheless, the second largest in New Zealand, and Central Otago is its hinterland, spreading from Taieri Ridge and the Strath Taieri west as far as the Southern Alps, and from the Hawkdun, Ida and Kakanui Ranges in the north to the Old Man, Old Woman and Umbrella Ranges in the south.

These mountains might look old, rounded and worn down by a rigorous climate. In geological timescale, though, they are surprisingly young, just five million years old in the case of the Hawkdun and Old Man groups, and a mere three million years in the case of the block-faulted central ranges (Rock and Pillar, Rough, Dunstan, Pisa and so on), which form a parallel pattern emanating from the Alps. Picture them as land waves, steep-sided on their eastern flanks, where faults are controlling their uplift. On their western side, they slope back more gently to an intervening valley.

The whole shooting match – the ranges and adjacent basins – are still going up, although only by a millimetre or two a year.

Whereas the mountains are relatively young, there are surfaces in Central Otago that go back a very long way – to a time, say, 20 million years ago, when the landscape was low-lying and a vast wetland of lakes and swamps and meandering rivers filled an area stretching from present-day Roxburgh to St Bathans. 'Lake Manuherikia' was subtropical, the home of crocodilians, snakes and eucalyptus trees, all now extinct. It had the look of Queensland. Did ancient mammals also once live here?

Some upland areas of Central Otago retain remnant old peneplain surfaces. Incredibly, the sea once invaded this landscape, at least as far as Naseby in the Maniototo. This happened, up to 20 times, in the Oligocene period, some 25 to 40 million years ago, when New Zealand was a collection of low-profile islands.

The landscape today bears no resemblance to those times. Nor does the climate, which is largely controlled by the rise of the Southern Alps to the west, where Mt Aspiring/Tititea, is the only mountain outside Aoraki/Mount Cook National Park over 3,000 metres in height.

Formed by uplift along one of the world's most conspicuous tectonic plate boundaries, the Alps are rising in the order of 10 to 20 mm a year, which is about the rate at which fingernails grow. In geological terms, this is meteoric. At the same time and at roughly the same rate, they are losing height by erosive processes powered by climate.

The Alps and the Fiordland mountains to the south form a wall that intercepts the moist airstreams advancing steadily eastwards across the Southern Ocean. The repercussions of this are two-fold: first, a West Coast environment that ranks as one of the world's wettest areas, where rainfall is measured in metres annually, and second, the creation of a 'rainshadow' region east of the main divide, largely protected from the worst of the wet weather. This region is Central Otago; hot in summer, cold in winter, and dry much of the year, a continental climate of sorts. Geographers describe it as semi-arid and subcontinental.

The driest place in New Zealand is the area around Alexandra. Here, rainfall is little more than 300 mm a year. As for cold, Central also holds the national record. On 3 July 1995, after several foggy sub-zero days, the temperature hit a metal-cracking minus 21.6 degrees Celsius at the old goldfield township of Ophir.

The region has known colder times still. Two and a half million years ago, when the Earth cooled and ice spread across the higher-latitude regions of the world in a series of ice ages, glaciers began carving future valleys, fiords and lake beds. Warm periods between the ice ages, lasting thousands of years, together with the presence of refuge areas in the landscape, allowed elements of the plant and animal life to survive, often through adaptation.

The alpine parrot kea of the western mountains, for example, evolved during the ice ages – an offshoot of its forest parrot relative, the kaka. Numerous new plants evolved to cope with the colder, higher environments, including some mountain daisies. A high proportion of New Zealand's endemic plants are found in the alpine zone, and in the ranges of Central as well as on the dry valley floors, the region claims its fair share of unique species.

Some areas are curiously salty and harbour specialised plant communities. There are mini-saltpans and areas of saline soils in various parts of Central Otago and South Canterbury – the only such features in New Zealand. At Sutton near Middlemarch is the country's only salt lake worthy of the name.

Further challenges to plant life and their associated insect and vertebrate communities are found on or near the summit crests, where extreme weather conditions have forced the vegetation to adopt the stature of tundra.

Towards Davidson's Top from near Lake Onslow

The Clutha Mata-au near Corbridge Downs

Central Otago in outline

In Central, age and dryness speak of an unchanging, timeless environment. Yet change is occurring naturally. From time to time, birds and winged insects are blown in from Australia. Among the avian newcomers are the spur-winged plover and white-faced heron, both of which colonised New Zealand from the south through the 20th century and are now common in Central. They will not be the last of the blow-ins.

Change has also been accelerated by human endeavour over the past few hundred years. The tussock grasslands owe their widespread distribution to the fires, deliberate or accidental, of early Polynesians and 19th century European pastoralists.

Maori were here for centuries, making seasonal journeys inland from settlements on the Otago and Southland coastline. They came for rock, notably argillite; for fibre, including Celmisia mountain daisy leaves and the dancing fronds of the ti or cabbage tree; and they came also for prized food such as eel, duck and pigeon, which they cooked on the move.

Europeans did not reach the Otago hinterland until 1853 – five years after the first Scottish settlers arrived in Otago Harbour aboard immigrant sailing ships. Twenty-two-year-old Nathanael Chalmers, with two Maori guides, was the first European to see Lakes Wakatipu, Wanaka and Hawea. Sick and exhausted by the arduous trek inland, he returned to the coastal lowlands down the Clutha River on a raft made of flax and raupo sticks, surviving the gorges and rapids.

The Clutha Mata-Au, still New Zealand's mightiest river, cuts straight through the middle of Central Otago from its outlet at Lake Wanaka, draining a main divide catchment stretching from the Haast Pass to the Routeburn. Here, then, is the ultimate landscape irony – a massive river eddying, swirling, sliding and tumbling through the nation's driest area.

At Lowburn, near Cromwell, the southward track of the Clutha is intersected by latitude 45 degrees south, the halfway point between the South Pole and the Equator. It is a landmark area in more ways than one, for Cromwell is the most inland town in New Zealand and the South Island at this point is at its broadest.

These are heartlands in every sense, natural, physical, human.

That Gilbert van Reenen loves to indulge himself in this landscape is self-evident. His images hum with the region's natural artistry . . . the sublime lighting and colour, the severe cold, the dry, treeless spaciousness, and the mountain majesty. Few people or human structures intrude into his images, and when they do, they speak of a backblocks landscape and experience, hard and character-building – and highly worthy of preserving.

His images provide an insight into the soul of Central Otago. Through them we commune with the region's special nature.

Water

Matukituki River delta and Mt Roy, Lake Wanaka

Previous spread: Morning light Roy's Bay and Eely Point, Lake Wanaka

Corner Peak, Lake Hawea

Lenticular cloud over Black Peak and The Peninsula, Lake Wanaka

North branch Wilkin Valley, Mount Aspiring National Park

The Sugarloaf at the 45th parallel, Lake Dunstan near Lowburn
Next page: Staircase Creek, Lake Wakatipu

Towards the Motatapu valley from Roy's Peninsula, Lake Wanaka

Blue Lake, St Bathans

Lake Castalia, Wilkin Valley, Mt Aspiring National Park
Previous page: The Routeburn at Forge Flat, Mt Aspiring National Park

Mt Alta and Lookout Hill from near the Matukituki outlet

Coronet Peak and Shotover River delta from near Queenstown Airport, Frankton

Earth

Schist Tors, Dunstan Range

Previous spread: Manuherikia Valley and Kakanui Range from near the Alexandra lookout

From the North Dunstan Range

Near the Lindis Pass

Ahuriri Valley near Ben Avon

Mt Awful and Lake Wanaka from near Isthmus Peak

Road to The Branches Station, Upper Shotover Valley

Summer shower near Shirlmar Station, Tarras

Winter light, Lindis Pass

First light near Phoebe Creek, Matukituki Valley

Upper Wye Creek, Remarkables Conservation Area

Last light on the Pisa Range above the Cardrona Valley

Atmosphere

Passing front, Roy's Peninsula and Mt Roy

Previous spread: Winter storm approaching, Minaret Bay, Lake Wanaka

Mou Tapu from behind Mt Burke

Towards the Remarkables and the Garvies from the Pisa Range

Schist tors and Old Man Range from Mt Dunstan

Nor'wester brewing over Mou Waho, Lake Wanaka

Next page: West from Mt Pisa

Equinoctial north west arch over Mt Alta

Sunrise on the Carrick Range near Duffers Saddle

Autumn, Ben Avon Tarns, Ahuriri Valley

Above the Crown Terrace and Kawarau River near Arrowtown

Autumn evening, Dublin Bay, Lake Wanaka

Tussocks and Grasslands

Glacial moraine hillocks and rural patchwork near Mt Barker

Previous spread: Red Tussock near Lake Onslow

Mt Alta and Mt Iron from near Mt Barker

Towards the Chain Hills from the North Dunstan Range

Nardoo Scientific Reserve, Te Papanui Conservation Park

Winter

Merino hoggets near the Hawkdun Range

Previous spread: Matukituki River mouth from Roy's Peninsula

Hawkdun Range from near the Ida Valley

Near the Lindis Pass

Rippon Vineyard and Ruby Island, Midwinter

Tititea and Mt Fastness from the Albertburn Saddle

Tititea (Mt Aspiring) from the south west

Overleaf: Merino ewes near Mt Barker

Lightscapes

Mt Aurum Reserve, Skippers Canyon
Previous spread: Winter light in the Ahuriri valley near Ben Avon Station

Spring flush, Dublin Bay, Lake Wanaka

Winter twilight near Lauder, Maniototo
Previous page: Double Cone on the Remarkables Range from the Wye Creek basin

Towards the St Bathans Range

High Cirrus over the Hawkdun Range

Acknowledgements
I am indebted to many people whose encouragement and advice have made my first book possible, particularly Robbie Burton, Geoff Chapple, John Hughes, Ros Herbison, Karina McLeod, Neville Peat, Lizzi Yates and Robyn van Reenen. To Andris Apse and Mike Langford, my sincere thanks for their supportive influence on my photography.

Technical information
Most of the panoramic images were created on transparency film using a Horseman field camera with custom-made (in Wanaka) Rodenstock lens mounts. The plates were scanned on an Imacon (Hasselblad) virtual drum scanner. Apart from minor corrections for aberrations, minimal manipulation has been carried out on the images. Specific locations of each image are located on page 6.

Archival prints
All images are available for purchase as signed archival prints on a range of media and in a variety of sizes, including large photo murals. Some are available as limited edition prints. For purchasing details please refer to www.cleangreen.co.nz

Stock photo library
The 66 original images in this book were selected from my searchable stock photo library of 25,000 unique, high resolution files of a wide range of subjects accumulated over 25 years. Usage rights to these images are available. Refer to www.vitalimages.co.nz for details.

Mail & bulk orders
Further copies of this book and my two other titles are available by mail order from Gilbert van Reenen, Clean Green Images Ltd, RD2, Wanaka 9382, New Zealand. Fax +64 3 443 7889 www.cleangreen.co.nz. Bulk order enquiries are welcome.

Photo safaris
Whenever possible, I like to share my favourite locations and knowledge with fellow photographers and artists. The tours are scheduled by arrangement and are tailored to suit the individual interests and experience level of participants. Refer www.cleangreen.co.nz for details.

Cover images
Front: Lammermoor Range Central Otago
Rear: Glendhu Bay from Roys Peninsula